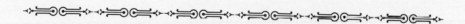

The Almanac for Desire

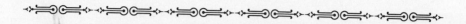

ALSO BY GARY FINCKE

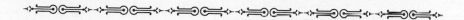

The Almanac for Desire

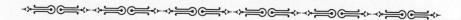

POEMS BY

GARY FINCKE

BkMk Press
The University of Missouri-Kansas City

BkMk Press
University of Missouri-Kansas City
5101 Rockhill Road
Kansas City, Missouri 64110-2499
bkmk@umkc.edu
(816) 235-2558 (voice); (816) 235-2611 (fax)

Financial assistance for this project has been provided by the
Missouri Arts Council, a state agency.

Book design by Roxanne Marie Witt
Cover image, "Princess Feather/Washington's Plume" (circa 1870),
          courtesy of the Ardis and Robert James Collection at the
          University of Nebraska (http://www.ianr.unl.edu/quiltstudy)

Library of Congress Cataloging-in-Publication Data

Fincke, Gary.
          The almanac for desire : poems / Gary Fincke.
            p.   cm.
          ISBN 1-886157-28-6
            I.   Title.

          PS3556.I457 A79 2000
          811'.54—dc21

                                        00-037860

Printed by Technical Communication Services, North Kansas City, Mo.

10   9   8   7   6   5   4   3   2   1

For Derek, Shannon, Aaron and especially, Liz

ACKNOWLEDGMENTS

American Literary Review, "The Agnes Mark"; *Colorado Review,* "Like She Was One of Us"; *Defined Providence,* "The Almanac for Desire"; *Doubletake,* "The Holy Numbers"; *Fine Madness,* "Arming the Bats"; *The Gettysburg Review,* "The Dark Angels"; *Hamline Journal,* "The Hitler Dance"; *The Laurel Review,* "Save, Economize, Repair, Arrange"; *Ledge,* "The Armstrong Scale"; *The Literary Review,* "Subsidence, Mine Fire, The Tomb of Eve"; *Mid-American Review,* "The Insulation of Steam" and "Light Enough to be Lifted"; *The Missouri Review,* "The End of Uncertainty", "The One Birds" and "Schmaltz"; *Oxford Magazine,* "The Dimpled Smiles of Mortal Dolls"; *Poet Lore,* "Chickens"; *Poetry East,* "The Solar-Powered Crematorium"; *Prairie Schooner,* "The Highway a Mile From Home"; *Press,* "The Repository of Transcribed Souls" and "The Spiritualists"; *Southern Poetry Review,* "The Personal Effects of Antiquity"; *The Southern Review,* "The Illustrated Life" and "Opening the Bone"; *Verse,* "The Natural Method of Dog Training"; *Weber Studies,* "The History of the Baker's Dozen"; *Zone 3,* "Baseball, Medicine, the English Major."

I

The Dark Angels

II

Save, Economize, Repair, Arrange

III

The Spiritualists

IV

The Natural Method of Dog Training

V

The Almanac for Desire

The Dark Angels

The Dark Angels

To the sidewalk in front of my father's
Razed bakery I return. To the patch
Of burdock where the stacked ovens deep-browned
The crusts of a million loaves and rolls.
To the cinderblock cracked like the soot-pocked
Windows where I watched, in Etna, the dark
Angels escape the coal smoke as if they
Wanted to swoop back to chimneys. To shards
And splinters where I hated the sauerkraut
In the cramped, next-door kitchen, the boiled
Shank end of pork which clustered flies against
The latched screen door. To the steep, shale
   downslope
Where the walls of the bakery are landfill,
Where the first bulldozed soil coats wallboard
And lumber as if coal were refueling
Industry's return, covering the spot
Where I was careless, once, with Saturday's
Trash fire. Where it followed the easy weeds
To the brittle boards of the bakery.
Where the neighbor shook free the flies and sprayed
His hose and a set of obscenities
Keyed to my foolish name. Where my father
Thanked him and led me to the last eclair,
Settled me on the work room's folding chair
And said nothing except "think," and I thought
That neighbor was listening at the window
While I held chocolate and custard until
My father said, "You eat that," and I did.

The Holy Numbers

We listened, as always, to Pastor Dave,
learning the Bible's major numbers, one
through the nine sixty-nine of Methuselah,
who lived eight times longer than all of us
put together. We memorized the three
parts of the Trinity, the four Gospels.
We recited the Ten Commandments
and the names of the twelve disciples,
subtracting Judas the Betrayer
before we matched them to the eleven
of ourselves, the future fishers of men.
Pastor Dave told us sacrifice stories,
the number of ways to be crucified,
including upside down, but the five boys
wanted to know the number of minutes
Jesus lasted on the cross, the number
of stones it took to slaughter Stephen.
Pastor Dave made us recite the Nicene
and the Apostles Creed, listening for
lapses because we were the future
of a faith which could spout, in unison,
the sixty-six books of the Bible,
ending with Revelation and its lists
of sevens and twelves. And I wanted
to ask the number of men who'd taken
Mary Magdalene to bed, and how much
she charged. And not asking, I counted,
on my own, the years I had until

three score and ten, learned the date for Easter
in 2015, when I needed
to rise from the dead and be repaid
for the 10% I'd been taxed by God.
Because I didn't see myself among
the nine groups blessed by Beatitudes,
not the boys who were poor in spirit;
not the meek we taunted; not the six girls
who were pure in heart, their bodies numbered
by breasts and thighs when the boys picked partners,
choosing until one was unchosen,
becoming the Virgin Mary, shifting
in her chair as if she were already
counting the two major heart attacks
of Pastor Dave, the three weeks between them,
the forty-two years he lived, including
the twenty-seven days after he laid
his hands to our heads and declared us saved.

Schmaltz

My mother's old bacon grease filled a jar
That sat among flour and sugar and salt
As if that unlabeled glass held one more
Kitchen staple. 100% fat,
100% thrift—the smoked flavor
Worked its way into eggs so we could eat
More meatless breakfasts. Or no eggs at all,
Just that grease, with green onions, reheated.
That meal took timing, taking the rye bread
To the barely hardened, sopping up *schmaltz*
Like uncles who drank coffee to cut it.
Such richness stayed overnight in the mouth
Where German melted into the English
Of memory, its sentimental schmaltz.
People my age were forgetting the waltz,
The fox-trot, and my father's sad box step.
What would be left, my mother worried, when
Conventional dances were gone? When thrift
Was laughed at? And all those warnings about
Salt and fat, the satisfaction of grease?
Already there were complaints about Heinz,
The soups my uncles made. Pittsburgh was home,
Now, to high blood pressure and heart disease,
All the Germans fleeing to the suburbs
Where bacon was drained, salt never slathered
On the crisped skin of chickens. My mother
Said we could shimmy it off in no time,

Doing the Twist and the Mashed Potato,
The dances of the slim who'd never heard
Of real *schmaltz* and the terrible success
Of learning place, those who wouldn't admit
To grandfathers who ate pure grease and lived,
Who'd punched in for fifty years and carried
The company's gold watch to prove it.

The Terrors

My mother, during the week,
Ended her stories in sorrow:
A house cleaned will be visited,
A house unkempt will live alone.
My aunt finished hers with fear:
The little boy's house got so dirty,
The neighbors burned it to the ground.
Outside were Stalin and the Rosenbergs,
The out-of-work and drunk, and those who
Suffered the great sin of shiftlessness.
There was a boy who saddened his mother
So often she turned into rain.
There was a boy who slept so much,
His mother buried him alive.
Outside was school where I'd follow
Directions or else, remember the maps
They had drawn and scaled for my walking.
A boy, once, had to live in a box
Because he forgot his way home from school.
A lost boy, at last, grew skinny
As straw and blew into a fire.
In the world of regret and anger,
Each of the women who waited
For me in first grade and day camp,
In Sunday School and the houses
Where music was taught by the half hour,
Had stories about boys who failed.

And so what? If I could read them,
They weren't about me; if every
Student could recite them, they were
No different than news, only public,
What the lettered world notices,
Not the personal, the terrors
We know variously in our hearts.

The History of the Baker's Dozen

Since he was twenty, for half of his life,
The baker has never shortweighted bread.
He accounts for the deception of air;
For cookies and cupcakes he gives thirteen.
But lately, there's been grumbling about size,
How his sweets are shrinking like candy bars.
And so much faith he has in the magic
Of numbers, how his customers are pleased,
He starts to box fourteen to the dozen.
A fool's shipment, an out-of-business count,
But his buyers gorge themselves on sweet rolls
Until everybody but the baker
Grows fat and wonders, "What's in it for him?"
While eating bear claws, the librarian
Learns the history of the baker's dozen,
All those extras insurance against fraud.
When nobody walks in to read, she calls
Her customers, and they nod from couches
As they lick thick icing from their fingers.
By now the baker only delivers,
Stops complaints at the front door with fifteen,
Then sixteen, stuffing his bargain-boxes
To pace the possibilities of guilt.
No matter the number, he's the thin man
The village hates as they wait, doors unlocked,
In their kitchens. He carries in twenty
For the price of twelve and they bad-mouth him.

When he brings them twenty-two, they curse him,
Oozing over their chairs like unwatched dough.
"Thief," they scream, "robber."   Those who stay
   in bed
Shout "Rapist, killer, bring that box in here."
By the evening he doubles their dozen,
They promise to kill him: "As soon as we
Lose weight," they holler. "As soon as you stop
Bringing us doughnuts." The baker can see
That each street where he delivers merges
With a freeway. He's sure no one he serves
Can squeeze inside a car, and the next night
He walks his route, pushing crullers and cakes
In a heavy cart. Just ahead of him
He hears howling. Beyond that is a roar.
"Lead us not into temptation," he says.
"How much powdered sugar will satisfy?"
Coming, at last, to thirteen times thirteen,
Calculating, recounting, beginning
To rise as if the end of gravity
Were the sweet blessing for the pure in heart.

Trinity Service

At the St. Barnabas Home, just before
The fundraising picnic, the destitute
And the crippled were led to be seated
In the middle section, so near the front,
All the summer visitors could watch them
Through the scripture readings and the shortened,
Outdoor sermon. There were men hunched over
To cough and spit, men strapped into wheelchairs,
Their free hands shaking with tics and palsies
And alcohol's delirious dry dreams.
There were men who sat upright in frayed shirts
And trousers once worn by the heavier
And taller, all watched over by black-robed
And hooded brothers as if they were bunched
For an enormous high school assembly.
In mid-June, a few of them would pass out
In the afternoon sun, and one would have
A seizure. They were our family, I heard
Each year, thankful to be sons and brothers.
And at the end of the Benediction,
Taped trumpets started "God of Our Fathers"
As the residents rose and retreated.
We faced forward. We finished every verse
While those men were locked down for the evening.
None of them carried cups of punch and plates
Of hors d'oeuvres to shaded benches and chairs,
But up three flights my mother's father lived

In a room where the branches of an oak
Clawed the window as if it were angry
He'd refused the church. "Can't make me," he said,
Spreading my mother's gift of Limburger
On a thick slice of onion, handing me
A buffalo carved from soap, offering
My sister a bear. "Wish me a whiskey,"
He said, the want that had driven him there.
He stroked his clip-on tie until it dropped
To the floor. "Snake," he whispered, sliding it
Toward my sister with his shoe. "Snake," he hissed,
Filling the window with his tight, white shirt,
All of us staring at the just-waxed floor
As if a miracle was being born.

The Dimpled Smiles of Mortal Dolls

My mother, forty years ago, refused
The Most Wonderful Story Doll, Jesus
In a gilded Bible watched over by
Cardboard cutouts of Mary and Joseph.
She shook her head like a million mothers
Who returned to the different darknesses
Of America's December. Ours was
Lit by the furnaces of Pittsburgh's mills
And occasional, fitful snow, but all
Of them, foreseeing the dogs that would chew
Off the arms and legs of Jesus, refused
Like unions until the toymakers bought
The Savior back from the country's dealers,
Each holy face of the Christ Child rendered
Into the dimpled smiles of mortal dolls,
Ones which wet themselves when they sucked upon
A bottle, ones which wailed when my sister
Turned them over her knee. Look, my mother
Wanted her daughter to love all her dolls,
Not awed by handling Jesus, not afraid
To drop Christ or, returning from phone calls,
Find him floating face down in the bathtub,
Teaching the terrible stillness of doubt.

The Solar-Powered Crematorium

There, in the demonstration, the body
Rose to the focal point of mirrors,
Stopped in sudden flame. The salesman said
We long to unite ourselves with the sun,
Not the hell of the common furnace,
And we stepped back, in the torched year
My mother died, to lift our heads
Like soldiers trucked near ground zero
To see the second sun of the A-bomb.
Such ashes we could carry, so much
Like draftees brushing the strange snow
From their bare arms, from their faces,
Walking it home regardless, to be
Opened later, nudged by fingertips,
Sifted, imagined back to its source
By the warm discoveries of touching.

The One Birds

Within the worst winter of the century,
I've started to foresee the sites for each set
Of drifts, the possibilities of sheer ice
On asphalt. I've had time, snowed in, to locate
The early signs of a dozen diseases
Which prove fatal, time to consider further
Examination and the self-serving prayer,
Both as likely as the drifts turning to waves
Which would crest and crash and wash away despair.

Twenty below, a black settling of feathers
On the mailbox, surely the obvious bad
Judgment of this morning, and I remember
The poorwill is the one bird that hibernates,
Sleeping in the cracks and crevices of rock.
I rouse myself with lift and throw, lift and throw,
And fine spray into my unprotected eyes
When the wind shifts, that unlikely bird sitting
Quiet as a vulture until I recall
The pale chanting goshawk, the one bird of prey
Which sings, celebrations possible for acts
We think would mute us, forcing apologies
From the faithless tongue: I'm sorry for the weeks
I've wasted, the years I've badly used. I'm loud
With remorse, and the bird, whatever its name,
Squawks and lifts large and heavy with survival
When I spike the plowed ice near the roadway, lift

A full load like someone who sees shoveling
As a way to heal the fatted heart, who is
Astonished, again and again, by bright sun
Which warms nothing, and by each of the one birds,
Like the mallee fowl, which, at birth, takes flight,
And is not surprised by its singular might.

Save, Economize,
Repair, Arrange

Save, Economize, Repair, Arrange

1

I didn't pack anything, this year, for Goodwill Industries.
I sorted shirts and pants and said NO. I refolded sweaters
And underwear and saw that everything was good.
Half a century I've lived, enough to feel like God choosing
Between the restarts of flood and fire, staying away,
Meanwhile, from the fatty meat of personal sacrifice.
I listen to myself like a doctor, use the instruments
Of my senses to make the simple diagnosis
Of apprehension. I want drawers so stuffed they cannot
    close;
I want every hanger clothed. Haven't I read the tags
On every purchase? Don't I know this lousy suit says
Fully Guaranteed for the Life of the Garment?
Good as new, I say, suddenly sure the cheap seams
In the crotch will split, the coat tear in the shoulder.
Good as new, yet I hold its awful stitching to the light
Of the window, the birds at the feeder fluttering up
And leaving me to myself behind the shimmering glass.

2

These days I'm impulse buying from the lot
Of used lives. I'm betting on the feel
Of kicked tires, the truth of odometers,
Convinced I can choose, though lately
I've listened to the stranger who says

He'll bet anyone he can bite his eye.
I've slapped my money on the wiped-down bar
To watch him put teeth to the popped bulb
And lay the false eye of silly choices
On my dollars like a paperweight.
"Remember," I hear my mother say,
"The revisions you promised yourself?
Begin with the prayers I taught you."
I lay awake, once, to listen for what
She'd ask from God, heard tread and sigh, creak
And rustle and my father's absence.
I rose, later, and opened, in the dark,
My closet, screaming to myself among
The armless stranglers until the light
Of reawakening switched on.
The one-eyed man stared at me and bet
He could bite his other eye. He read
The numbers on the cash register
Where the price of my last drink was posted,
And I cupped that wobbling eye, doubled
My bet before he spit out his teeth,
Lifted them to his smiling face,
Set them exactly on the socket.

3

My mother, in heaven, is happily saving,
So many years, still counting, the principal joy
Of her paradise. She's storing hand-me-downs;
She's fixing things and promising to slip back
Through the needle's eye with her heavenly tools

To keep me from the foolish bets of disbelief.
Save, economize, repair, arrange, she says,
So clear she might be breathing again to tell me.

Something is always on the fritz,
Gone kerflooey—appliances,
Necessities with moving parts,

The furnace in January
During this snow skidding sideways
Through the tunnel of the breezeway.

My mother's heart. Her expressions
For the way machines work
And the world according to God.

Absence aligns itself like tools
Sized to wrench anything apart.
Fix something, fix something, I say

Like an all-night drip. Fix something—
The gibberish of instructions
Draining down the page of numbered steps.

Electricity. Oil. Gas.
I try the foreign language of fuel,
The one with no verbs, and listen

For translations to heat and light.
The wiring in these walls speaks
The Esperanto of disrepair.

Every one of these switches turns
Flexible as tongues and forces
Air across the chords of darkness.

4

When I left, everything I'd ever worn
Filled four drawers plus thirty-six marked boxes,
And I returned, thirty years from college,
To madras and window pane and pin stripe;
To white Levis so deeply creased they knelt.
Nothing had vanished, not briefs and t-shirts.
That room had become a great retelling,
Speaking like the Neanderthals' cave

In France where rows of iron pyrite, ordered
By size, still sparkle forty thousand years
After the final rearrangement.
Like van Heurn, the biologist, who pinned moles,
Hundreds of skins flattened, splayed, and facing
The one way he selected. And then pigs,
Nose out and ears up; and dogs open-mouthed,
None of them misplaced in the caverns
Of his collections, composing like
My mother who died and left five hundred
Planters' labels rolled and rubberbanded
For discount dishes, a thousand clipped
Panels from General Foods to trade
For flatware. Who stored two hot water tanks
And four upright vacuum cleaners. Who shelved

Seven toasters, eleven radios,
And three televisions tuned to clouds,
Waiting as if that personal landfill
Would follow her soul, junk as faith,
The hope-chest cellar stuffed with trash.
"Just you wait," she'd say, "you never know,"
Accumulating like the man who boxed

The brain casts of squirrels, chickens, tigers
And bears to build an evolution
Theory, speculating by size. She said
The sun is scheduled for extinction,
The moon drifts away from us by inches
Per century. And now, in the museum
Of futures, so many numbers lie left
Of the decimal, we slip the darkness
With the code of chronology,
The chant of relative importance,
Gathering like Pharaohs believing
We'll sort it out, later, when we have time,
When there's an eternity of leisure
To order and classify what filled
Our cartons and caves, our cellars and crypts.

The Spiritualists

The Spiritualists

On television, this evening, stories
Of premature births, an astonishment
Of medical miracles, the problems
Which follow—children crippled, babies
Precarious with pneumonia, deaths
Of the weakest, like the son of a friend
Who showed slides, one night, each of them
Seconds apart in sequence during
The first day of a forty-hour life.
He spoke for himself and his silent wife,
Explained complications and symptoms,
The inevitability of loss.
And the last of those pictures, a head shot,
Stayed through his story of heaven,
How families were reunited,
Keeping me quiet about the woman
Who painted the face of a lost infant
On her breast, who sat in a cabinet
In the dark and waited for parents
To accept the possibility
Of contact. Who spoke to the departed.
Who bared the beautiful face
Of their dead child and thrust it through
The shadowed, sized opening
Into the dim light for viewing. Who asked
Joyful parents to extend their hands
To brush the soft faces of their children,
Repeating the name of the resurrected,

What I couldn't do, even then,
Staring at the lost, cyanotic child,
Thinking of reassurances,
The roll calls for the briefly living,
What forces us back to simple light.

Subsidence, Mine Fire, The Tomb of Eve

For the thirty-third year of the Centralia mine fire.

In the *Encyclopaedia Britannica*,
For three editions, paragraphs
About the Salem Church Dam, height
And length, the power and purpose
Of the never-constructed because
Some fact-checkers believed it built,
That a reservoir had risen behind it
So long ago the water was true.

Like hell ready for the day of moving,
Like the huge hole which opened
Outside my classroom window and stopped
Three feet short of the brickwork wall.
Coal mine, certainly. Underground fire.
But for all I knew, the sudden suck
Of collapse would widen to the ribbons
And sawhorses, the students and teachers
And the first crush from the neighborhood
Pressed near the great vandalism of chance.
I told myself to turn away before
The windowsill leaned out and down,
The earth swallowing in its ancient way,
Forecasting like the Mother of Mankind,
Who spoke, in Jedda, for thirty years
From the tomb of Eve. She took questions
Through a slim shaft to the original dead,
So far underground, so many coins fed
By foreign pilgrims, she listened

For tone and accent to prepare
The exact change of the answer to send
Up the pneumatic tube for hope.

There were those who trembled with lust,
Those who offered themselves to her, what
They were willing to do or have done,
Buying queries of blood and semen.
There were those who tunneled until
She used the backdoor to escape
From the warren of secret wants.

And how long should I walk, this morning,
Where traffic is banned? What questions, years
After that school collapsed, should I shout
Through this highway split, finally, from
That mine fire's arrival? What prophecies
Might I hear, following the fire's
Old fissures through the cemetery,
Laying my hands to the smoldering earth

Near the church where the sinkholes plummet
To seams burned back to simmering?
Who answers for the future?
In the neighboring field rise rusted rows
Of vents, and no smoke escapes from any,
Moved on, the world beneath them ash.

The Repository of Transcribed Souls

*The first autopsy in the New World
was done to determine whether
Siamese twins had one soul or two.*

Now that the Siamese twins had died,
now that they were opened by the saw
of the surgeon, the priest prepared
to do the autopsy count for souls.
Which space in the rib cage permitted
the soul to flee? Which emptiness
behind them was sized by absence?

Here, this morning, I'm shown the sealed drawers
of the monument where a part
of my family lies hidden an inch
from the sun, avoiding the grave
and the slab of the mausoleum.

A dozen names, not ours, fill three sides
of the squared base, all of them etched
like the memories of those who record
everything they know on floppy discs for
the repository of transcribed souls.

There, in alphabetized files, their thoughts
are waiting for the heavenly hands
of a clerk to extract them, downloading
a billion bytes of memory,
their voices droning down a purchased screen
among the infinite in paradise.

The Agnes Mark

Hurricane Agnes, in the early 1970s, drove
the Susquehanna River to a record flood.

My son wanted the thunderstorm turned down
Like a radio. He asked me where
The knobs were, the great handles for God
Who could fix clouds or repair wind through wires
To weather. I'd told him the secrets
Of magic, where the tricks were hidden
For ascending ropes and levitated
Women, and now he wanted to cross
The Susquehanna stone to stone where
We walked it weekly like geography's
Linemen, confirming it so open
And shallow all summer, I repeated
The story of Jimmy Karas, who drowned
While fishing in Pine Creek where you could wade,
Except after heavy rain, from one side
To the other, where no one would fish
Except in the deepest pools, where you
Couldn't drown unless you fished alone
And fell and struck your head; and my son
Nodded at circumstance as if he
Were memorizing another set
Of times tables or the number of steps
A student of mine had fallen, hitting
Her head exactly where the brain shows
Its vital stem. For that awful luck,
I'd said I'd tumbled down stairs, wooden
And carpeted and cement, nine times,

And broke nothing except tooth and skin,
Though nobody else, as far as I knew,
Had drowned in Pine Creek or Penn's Creek, where
We'd crossed before the rain a hundred yards
From its end in the Susquehanna
Where thousands, I repeated, had drowned.
The truth was he knew I was frightened
Of water the way I was afraid
Of heights, that I feared so many things
I wasn't to be trusted with advice
On danger. I was wrong about water
And the qualities of buoyancy.
My stories featured only the dead:
There'd been so much rain in January,
So shortly after the heavy snow,
The river rose past each recorded stage
But the Agnes Mark, stalled my friend's car
So suddenly it seemed terrified
To go on. It squatted, door open,
In the channel of his river road,
And nobody had the strength to close it.

Opening The Bone

The morning of my operation,
I read the history of trepanning,
How skulls, for eight thousand years,
Have been drilled to lessen the bone.
The world's oldest medical
Procedure, the book said, but the night
Before, a student I knew had been
Bludgeoned with fists and shoes, his skull
Opened by an older treatment.
At the dentist's, set for surgery
That would break bone to put an end
To pain, I read a set of sayings
From dentists past: "A frog tied to the jaw
Can make teeth firm" from the Romans.
"A live mouse held to the gums stops toothache"
From the Egyptians. Culture by culture
They offered cures, and I looked for
The nostrums of the drunk and brutal,
Checked for the names of the vicious
Who have taken the teeth of victims
With the simple assault of anger.
And there, just before the sign sank
To shadow behind the bowed head
Of a woman who was waiting
For her own oral corrections was
"Scratch painful gums with the teeth of a man
Who has died violently," but I
Could not see who was given credit

For that prescription, not even when
I rose, for my standing straightened her
In her chair as if she thought my hands
Were the animals of bad advice.

Light Enough To Be Lifted

Each evening, after dinner, from April
To October, my neighbor weeds his lawn
By hand. So it's perfect, he says,
Chemical-free, throwing one arm toward
Three treated lawns we face. I keep trim,
He says, by stepping outside before drinks
Or dessert, and he leaves me to sum the pounds
He's never added through the discipline
Of hands in the soil, to think of the woman
Who aborted her fetus so she'd be
Light enough to be lifted to heaven
During the Rapture. Of the man who built
A life-sized Jesus from toothpicks, counting
The square, the round, the flat and sandwich kinds
To sixty-five thousand separate sticks.
What weight of needs we carry. What fat so
Difficult to trim we butcher ourselves
With beliefs. I look down where the first thread
Of plantain might show itself, imagine
Seed and spore, the tangle of conception.
Below the earth, in Texas, this country
Has stored thirty-two billion cubic feet
Of helium. Just in case. Starting with
The threat, once, of possible blimp warfare,
Continuing through the astonishing
Catastrophes of the surface which lifts
As if the Rapture for inanimates
Were beginning, all the beautiful things
Soaring toward the heaven for possessions.

The Armstrong Scale

Descending into Italy from the Alps,
Traveling down the only cliff's edge trail,
Hannibal had enormous rocks to move.
His men cut trees. Heaped the logs and set fire
To those boulders. There, still high enough
For summer snow, they poured vinegar
Over the seething stones and went to work
With picks. Elephants milled in the drifts,
Thousands of soldiers shuffled and shivered
While that vinegar softened the stone because
They knew nothing about the dynamite way
To widen roads. Though still, when I'm snagged,
First in the long line of idling cars, I stand,
Astonished, with the flagman to watch
A blast tear away the stones which slow us.
"You can see the cliff's changes from the moon,"
He tells me, "because it's bigger than
What Armstrong saw—The Great Wall of China,"
And after the tumble of a truck's worth
Of rocks, I follow the dust that drifts east
Toward the river which started this highway.
A dragon, according to legend, marked
The path of the Great Wall, leaving his footprints
For forced labor to follow. In the end,
After thousands of miles, the builders
Had planned so well there was only one brick
Left over, not this rubble near a river,
Which can be seen, by the Armstrong scale,

From the moon. Nearby, the Amish pull boulders
From the ground by hand. Along the shoulder
Where we stand, they drive through this pass by horse
And buggy, traveling so slowly they might
Be seen from the golden moons of heaven.

Chickens

Ten thousand chickens, my friend owns,
This ward of them using the great weapon
Of dust when they flutter, then settle
From our interruption. I'm lightheaded
From the dung and mold, giddy enough
To think of Nancy Luce, who inscribed
Her poems on the eggs she gathered,
Adding the names, after she'd finished,
Of the chickens who'd laid those tablets.
Dedications perhaps, like Psalms
In praise of the hens she raised.

She talked like a magician, the woman
Who told me this tale, rolling up
Her empty sleeves, waving her arms where
Levitation's cheap strings could have hung
From her henhouse rafters. Her stories
Wove webs through the flooded air;
Her hands spun brown eggs from beneath
The two-note protests. She could have been
A widow selling off an edge of farm,
Not spieling the patter of distraction,
But she said "Watch—keep watching," and I
Kept my eyes on her hands while she lifted
An axe and swung, the hen doing
The headless scuffle before dropping
By the door to end the old trick

Of usefulness. Now they're dust and squawk,

And I say nothing about fresh eggs.
Now they're a threat of beaks, the working parts
Of me turning foolish while I listen
To the whistle of retreat from my lungs.
Inhaler, I wish, settling for gasps
On the grass outside. Mary Bateman,
That widow added, found *Christ is Coming*
On the eggs laid by her chosen hen.
God, she said, had told her to expect
Fourteen days of eggs with words, followed
The next morning by judgment's firestorm.
"No time to waste," she said, to pay her
For a guaranteed pass to heaven.

Her neighbors, shaken by the second day's
Coincidence, pondered. On the third day,
One more *Christ is Coming* drove them
To settle sensibly with the Lord.
Pilgrimages began. The arrivals
Of those who could pay for salvation.
Heaven, like countries, had border guards,
Angels who stamped your hand if you showed
Proper papers. And suspicion?
What's to gain on the short countdown
To hereafter? Who would begrudge
Mary Bateman heaven's extra comfort,
What wealth might buy in the sky?

And surely the skeptical doctor,
On the fourteenth day, brought money
With him just in case the earthly ink
On each egg was one more instance

Of God's mysterious use of doubt.
And when the doctor dared investigate,
When he broke the privacy of hen
And owner, he heard the great squawkings
Of miracle's pain, the final,
Altered egg being forced, by hand,
Back along the path from which it came.

Think of timing, how a few more minutes
Would have God's medium reloaded.
There, Mary Bateman could have said,
The last egg, gathering shillings
During the rest of Earth's final day.
Think of the supernatural light
Of the following morning, the sun
Spotlighting the crowded village.

Think of the concurrent prayers running
Up the beam like extraordinary
Telegrams of gratitude. Think of all
Salvation's shareholders sitting down
To a final feast, making the noises
My family raises on holidays,
The celebrations of the tongue and hands
While we ring the three chickens
And their three stuffings of fruit
And bread and sausage to suit
Our differences after we've gnawed
The browned-early appetizers
Of gizzards and livers and hearts.
After the text of preparation,
The reading of hunger, we are left

With blood and muscle, gravies thick
And thin to pass until we share
The salted skin and the ritual toast,
The list of remembrances, the praise
For safe travels, and the swift prayer
Against futures like the ones
I wish for these chickens, waiting
In the sun while my friend finishes
Whatever he must do regardless
Of why I'm absent, whether I'll explain
It only takes such dust a minute,
As fast, for my lungs, as plutonium.
Whether I'll say I still have faith
In the three drugs I wear for ambush,
That nothing is ending here
But my concentration on breath.
That absent trill and warble, these flocks
Cough up the notes which do not move us.
That I hope he slaughters all of them
For a county's worth of celebrations.
That I want the defense of good eating,
Not one mention of messengers
From the fortuitous barnyard,
Nothing about the resurrection dream
Of the chopping block, blood's fantasy,
The magic of the plucked and hung
So strong he will wrap a dozen hearts
And livers, and when I eat them,
I will remember all of the flesh
I have swallowed or touched, so rich
In salt and butter I could be
Preparing myself for paradise.

The Natural Method
of Dog Training

The Natural Method of Dog Training

"Torture, which was once a craft, has become a technology."
                                        Dr. Timothy Shallice

1

My mother said, "Accept no rides from strangers.
Don't even approach an unfamiliar car."
My father told me his search-party story,
The naked boy found, too late, tied to a tree.
The tongue was pulled from his throat; the lines
        still breathe:
"You never catch those drivers," my father said,
Yet I stood at the roadside, thumb extended,
And he swerved at me so suddenly I took
The guardrail with the step and leap of panic.

2

To teach, according to the slim manual
For *The Natural Method of Dog Training*,
You lay tacks on the furniture, covering
The forbidden places for sleep. You throw
Firecrackers from your moving car to keep
That dog off the road. You spray it with a hose.
You place rat traps among the roses where
Digging's not allowed. And when nothing
works,
You starve the animal to show who's boss.
It will come begging, then, apologetic
And compliant. You will own a well-trained dog.

3

When the general came to our school,
When he lectured us at the assembly
About the A-bomb and the safety
Of America, he called radiation
"Cloudshine" to honor the sky's pink glow.
One teacher, when the science fair,
Arrived, told us a girl in Utah,
The year before, brought the head and neck
Of a cow for her exhibit, those parts
Split open to show the tumors
Which had murdered her father's herd.
In another part of the country,
A man hypothesized hormesis,
The therapy of low-level rads
To toughen us toward longer lives.
Pantywaist, sissy, mama's boy—
We were still using, to cure cowardice,
The old therapy of namecalling.
Pansy, fairy, faggot, queer—
The double-dare of the schoolyard
And boot camp made it easier
To gut than go home, to shoot than say NO.
Trial and error. School of hard knocks.
We cry or don't cry. We grin and bear it
Or we scream and run. No pain, no gain,
We put our fingers to the flame;
We lay them on the coils just after
The red fades. So our lives will be better,
So we can distinguish right from wrong
And be numbered among the saved.

4

Once upon a time, doctors pulled the foreskin
Over the tip of the penis, punched holes
And stitched it to prevent masturbation.
That will do for now, they said to parents.
He'll think twice or pay the penalty
Of pain for allowing sin's tumescence.
There were remedies, from the beginning,
For every carnal crime, including
The natural method of castration,
So effective, so long, it was used
On epileptics and the insane.
Weren't seizures just sexual release?
Didn't the original sin of sex
Propel the weak to mental illness?
"The most significant factor
In social reform in history"—
One expert declared as the era
Of the electric chair began,
Civilization about to
Be rid of capital crimes.

5

In the history of aversion therapy,
In the celebrated cases when cures
Were claimed, the physicians always speak:
Like Alexander Morrison, the champion
Of camphor oil, his patients swallowing
Their way to sweating and vomiting,
Diarrhea, convulsions. "That does it,"

He said, publishing his lectures to acclaim,
How he followed the progress of nine men
Who practiced "the crime against nature."
The way they took their dose with the sight
Of naked men. The way two of them changed,
Or so they said, cured of one kind
Of insanity. The way the lust
Of seven was so severe they stayed
Aroused, near-death, by anything male.
Like John Wesley, who ministered
With the electric friction machine
To save the worst of his Methodist flock.
"The unparalleled remedy," he said,
Preaching the gospel of therapy
As if it were one more metered phrase
For a hymn, the one in progress while
He watched the hair rise on the lunatics
Of little faith, those who might be rescued
From hell by small bolts of holiness,
Something like the practices of Saint Rose,
Who wore a chastity belt for life,
Who threw away the key and daily
Whipped herself. Who ate poisons, then fasted
Near death. Who disfigured herself. Who wore
A hair shirt and a crown of thorns. Who dragged
With her a wooden cross, preceding
Saint Marina, not outdone, who added,
To her belt, spikes and iron teeth.

6

In one test, snails were fed a food

They'd never tasted, given two hours
Before sickened by injection.
Always, after that, they refused
That dinner, even weeks later,
A long stretch for the memories
Of snails. And surely the patients
Who vomit recall, outstripping
The snails, memorizing like birds
Who retrace the migration paths
Or die; like deer who recollect
The proper winter trails or starve.
In California, in the late Sixties,
In the state hospitals at Vacaville
And Atascadero, patients were
Softened by Anectine, overdosed,
With or without a medical release:
Complete paralysis, breathing stopped
For three minutes, subject still conscious,
The better to be conditioned by
The suggestions of the doctors.
"An extremely negative experience."
One witness said, yet those sex offenders,
Those criminally insane, were told,
When released, the do-it-yourself
Therapies of snapping rubber bands
Against their wrists, shoving fingers
Down their throats when unorthodox
Sex thoughts began. And, for tough cases,
The do-it-yourself of a shock machine
Made portable. "Useful in the playground"—
How the catalogue put it while I was
Busy with monkey bars and swings,

All that playground metal conducting
Improved behavior through my childish frame.
That did it, not the collective shock
Which worsened us, not the sad siren
Of civil defense, the tight tuck
In the stairwell, or the sprawl behind
The green dumpster when caught outside.
For improvement, you needed to be
Singled out, to cry where everyone
Could see you, every wail as visible
As a stain spreading from the crotch.

7

So late in December, so cold
across the full width of Ohio,
I was working up the self-pity
of "casualty," equating myself
with the sleepers on sidewalks.

So long between rides, I skipped
pre-scanning the driver to see
what he might charge, a policeman,
the car unmarked, or a man
in uniform aroused by boys.

I used classroom diction. I kept
eye contact with the highway,
the border five miles away. And when
we passed the welcome sign, not slowing,
I thought I was a sadist's dream.

In Pennsylvania, where I was
heading, a man had entered the homes
of women with a store-bought badge.
He let them live to be witnesses,
all six repeating boots and blue hat,

the dark-brown holster, none of them
remembering a face. "You know you're
illegal," he said, while I studied
chin and nose, a scar below the ear.
"If I choose," he said, "I'll make you pay."

Two days to the new year, that car
unheated to keep him up, I poured
the night sweats of the terminal.
He listed bus and train, the relative
safeties of ticketed rides.

Outside, ambiguous snow swirled up,
then cleared. He said he had pictures
of a boy flung into a landfill,
the work an overnight of rats
can do. He said "Look under the seat,"

and I didn't. He said "End of the line,"
slowed, and the animals of evening
said nothing while I filled the door.
They might have been listening for
the sweet groans of dawn while he u-turned,

while he opened his window and drove
the soft shoulder like a mailman
to deliver a photograph
which brushed me, then fluttered between
his tire tracks, face down like choice.

8

Throughout high school, story after story
About radiation sickness, the short
And long term of it in Nevada
And Utah, testimonials from
Survivors about a smorgasbord
Of cancer and government denials.
And one story, finally, about
The benefits of uranium, how
It pulls diseases from the body,
Sending patients into played-out mines
For the cure of the abandoned cave.
And then a rush of precedents, including
The claims of Elisha Perkins,
Who held a patent on The Tractor,
Two rods which drew disease from the body
By the mix and alignment of alloys,
How they were held, lowered and raised
Like the palms of Christ or the surrogates
Who placed their healers' hands and prayed
At sunrise service, telling the tumors
To follow the sun. And there were
Testimonials, a neighbor's breast
Restored, an uncle's tumor shrunk.
And whether those old recoveries

Proved those rods responsible,
Whether cure lasted for hours or years,
George Washington, for one, believed,

Bringing his family to the early version
Of the uranium cure, though he was bled,
Just before death, by his doctors,
Submitting to basic extraction,
What could be verified, not
The possible pull of alloys, not
The wishful benefits of the unseen.

9

Coach said to drink no water
during practice. We'd cramp,
he said, and water guzzlers
were losers who would run
from battle. He'd witnessed
foxhole fear, the piss and moan
of cowardice. There was war
waiting for us in Asia,
and nobody on this team
would do less than good, he'd see
to that, fifteen laps, fast breaks,
a scrimmage, and the night
he switched us into darkness,
lit flares in four corners
of the gym. You keep that ball
moving, he said. You take it
to the hole and crash those boards,
firing his starter's pistol,

advancing while we screened
and rolled, moved without the ball,
more than ready, he said,
to invade any school
who thought "battle-tested"
was just a chalk-talk phrase.

10

After the expanded war stripped
our student deferments, we sold
self-pity in the flea market
of the dispossessed, borrowing
lake front for beer and girls we hoped
to seduce with new-world sorrow.
By summer we'd be refugees,
selected so low by lottery
we'd lug a small part of ourselves
to a bus and listen for rules.
Those girls would finish college or not,
but that day one of them coupled
so close, so much in a clearing,
we thought she'd pull a train of soldiers.
One of us walked our proposal
forward like a diplomat, that girl
so still I thought my friend had killed her.
I heard "all yours," numbers up to six,
my voice assigning my place in line.
Suddenly, each of the other girls smoked.
The sky became a two-way mirror.
As if heaven were behind it, I stared,
repeating what I'd bid on, turning

away, drinking and looking across
the water as if glare were important.
I could see better with my back turned,
remembering dogwood, the burgundy
of that blanket, the fraternity crest
centered under her passive thighs.
I erased dandelions with my shoes.
And when I heard Number Six walk away
I didn't flinch, so he could have left
or helped that girl, because when I turned,
finally, the empty space had reformed
among those sweet-scented, flowering trees.

11

A week later, a whore in Cleveland
asked me what I wanted for ten dollars,
whether I was scared or queer, hesitant
in Hough, where race riots were months away.
I was playing my last tournament
tennis for a church-related college.
The next morning I would lose my match
to the one black player in the conference,
and what was I accomplishing
with my doubles partner, the two
of us so white outside the blues bar
we festered like pimples shut up
by stupidity and cowardice.
I said there was nothing she could do
worth ten dollars, said it so measured
and clear to myself that my partner
agreed when I stepped off the curb,

skittering beside me the three blocks
back to where the races mixed, then,
more slowly, three more to where we slept.
"Edison Medicine," I said, quoting
the one person I'd met who'd been sent
to shock treatment. "Look here," he'd murmured,
so softly and so soon after
he'd picked me up, I thought he'd opened
his pants or his set of photographs
would feature nude boys, not Edison's
early film, the electrocution
of an elephant. Didn't I know
the first electric chair was built
at Menlo Park? Didn't I know
they tested dogs and horses and cows
before the first prisoner took minutes
to literally cook? Didn't I see
my body as meat? "You look in the back,"
he said, "and guess," and I swiveled,
saw milk cans, and said nothing at all
while he described the explosions
they'd make if we wrecked or tore through
the wrong Ohio pothole. I was
considering the crimes of elephants
and the ones I'd been lately committing.
"Has you thinking, doesn't it?" he said,
right about that, offering beer
with the early warning of attack,
making me think of opening my door
like a school bus driver each time
we reached a set of railroad tracks.
I didn't ask out. I didn't ask for

the next bottle from the six pack
between the worn seats, tough enough
to flee Youngstown, Ohio, with
the cargo of possible bombs.
Just before my school, the neighborhood
turned to bones. Forty minutes I'd worked
to ask no questions. In two more,
I knew the pedestrians I'd meet,
the likely rides if I decided
to leave again. Behind barbed wire
one night shift had parked a lot full.
Pretend you're driving to work, I said
to myself, imagining I could use
the machinery inside those walls,
identical sculptures lurching by
on black, rubber belts, all of us
busy with building the one thing.

12

Now I can buy a video filmed
From a dog's point-of-view, the camera,
Apparently, two feet from the ground,
The subjects those a dog should love:
A duck chase, car rides, a cattle roundup.
"A tape," the brochure claims, "your dog can watch
Over and over," twenty-five minutes
A long time for my dog to watch
Anything unless I train her,
Unless she knows to stay put, flattened
Against the car floor when we cross gravel,
What she hears at the kennel, at the vets.
The way my first son, not quite two,

Screamed when the signal flashed to turn
Left at the apartments because
He knew what that babysitter did
Before his seven-hour shift expired.
Now I can tour the ninety-nine test sites
Of Yucca Flat, hear the anecdotal
Evidence of poisoning dismissed.
Now the theory of hormesis says
Chernobyl will save lives, condition
The Russians like an invisible coach.
And now I'm offering one story
About pathfinding, how I learned
The clues of crossed sticks, the secrets
Of stones arranged into landmarks
In the manual I memorized,
The troop so far ahead nothing
Of them remained but symbols.
Now I'm learning the Roerich sign,
Three dots triangular in
A circle to protect against
Destruction. I'm turning wishful
Among hex signs for caution
Of every degree, something like
The tripled sticks or stones which warn
Comprehensively of danger:
Quicksand, cliff, poison ivy, wasps—
Simplicity's hope, not the demands
Of perpetual poison, something
Cartographers of the toxic need
For the long trip to the future.
Fifty thousand years, durable
As plastic, their signs must signify

The shriek of STOP. Reconvened,
The Voyager Committee tests
Symbols for flying to aliens
At the far end of half-lives.
Consider them children, they're told,
Who find inexplicable etchings;
Consider them Scouts who would flee
The permanent gesture for danger.
Or else they will gather for the slow
Levering of rock, the unscrewing
Of threads, waiting to see what will
Be lifted to the light, what might scream
Through the noise of insects, the shifting
Of dust, the chatter of elements
Emitted from a billion tongues
Like legacy's Esperanto.

The Almanac for Desire

The Almanac For Desire

Today you stop so often
At the same comma, you brush
The page for the braille
For failure. Today you see
Each phrase followed by end stops,
None of them naming the want
Of fingers, the need of tongue.
The drapes sieve the afternoon;
The strained light covers your hands
With the gauze of cataracts,
Turning them vague as surprise.
In the almanac for desire,
Each month shows four phases
Of sin; in one, the blue moon
Of the irretrievable.
The worn rug of second thoughts,
Twilled into brief highways,
Brings a finger to the bell,
A package which skids when you
Force open the door, pitches
So easily onto its side
You believe it holds the future.

The Illustrated Life

At Woolworth's, in Pittsburgh, one counter
showed seventy feet of Davy Crockett—
telephones, t-shirts, and six fat stacks
of coonskin caps—but all I owned were
the cards I counted, from Tennessee
to the Alamo, and a lunchbox
I carried January to June,
memorizing all the verses to
the three-minute ballad by Bill Hayes.
By summer, Eisenhower sported
a Crockett tie, and I'd never say
another word about frontiersmen
or wanting to own a silly hat.
From front to back, across the nave,
and up again to the panel
nearest the altar, Jesus lived
and died and rose once more to glory
in the stained glass windows of our church.
In my room, I had a three-foot shelf
for Christ—Bibles, a hymnal, and books
of instruction for Lutheran boys.
His ministry was full of prone
and kneeling men. Even the faces
of the standing tilted up at him.
Along each pew, men and women
sealed offerings in envelopes
as if our congregation were
bidding, in a silent auction,

on eternity. Always, on clear
Sundays, Christ's early years were brightened
by morning sun, pillars of light
ascending toward a hint of wings.
After prayer and the benediction,
after amen and a hymn, I rushed
to radio and television
to memorize their promises for
my years to come. In the next panel
my body muscled. In the next
I fought and fumbled along an aisle
lined with stained-glass pictures of pleasure,
even if I had to bid and pay,
even if the panels stayed dark
and earthbound from dawn to dusk.

Arming The Bats

The white shirts spoke answers to the questions
Which hollered from the console radio.
Would Kruschev launch? Kennedy bluff us dead?
There were two pilots and a tail-gunner
In those chairs: Germany, Korea, SAC.
One uncle knew the weight of the A-bomb,
The exact radius of readiness.
One aunt cloved a brown-sugared ham; one brought
Green tumblers of root beer and shook her head
As if she knew his cancer was tracing
The great arc of the ballistic missile.
"You build them, you use them," her husband said.
A toy football lurched off my lap and rocked
Three seconds of silence through the rec room.
It lay quietly through one pilot's tale
Of the secret plan for bats, how hundreds
Were dropped, carrying napalm, from a plane
To test one more way to destroy Japan.
It didn't matter, he said, that the bombs
Were too heavy, because most of those bats,
As usual, were sleeping, and tumbled
To earth like humans. The radio switched
To music; that uncle said survivors
Flew to the nearest available caves
And burned the airport's hangars. He picked up
The football and added, "That plan was scrapped,
May, 1943, handing the war
To science." And then he tossed that rubber

At the brother who'd lifted and landed
The A-bomb while an aunt shouted "ready"
So loudly she might have intended to
Summon the family next door to dinner.

The Highway a Mile From Home

No one believes in the skid marks
On the pavement. They disappear
Like the cop's chalked body outlines.

What I remember of the car's
Madness is how the side window
Filled with green. That impossibly

It burst and parted, shivering
Away from the space I was filling.
That I thought about opening

The door. That surely I was not
Sharing all that regretted speed.
I turned into a child who knew
The world's worst demons had found him,

Smearing the thin tread of my voice
Across the slick, black floor of that
Highway, and I heard it start, huge,
Breathless silence that blinds the heart.

Baseball, Medicine, The English Major

In the school film the man who was
Given one wish lay sick beside
His treasure. He wished and wished,
Too late, for health, while we whispered
Our wishes for home runs or shutouts
Along the dugout of our desks
Until the lights, suddenly, switched on,
And we were freeze-tagged by the nurse,
Twisted and turned and reversed.
"Boys," she said, "I swear you're possessed.
You've all got the St. Vitus' Dance."
We laughed. We started twitching
Like batters digging in for curveballs.
She could have called our teacher
To cast out the devils in us,
But she rewound the film, said nothing
About its foregone conclusion,
And closed the door on our dancing.

The first time I saw chorea,
I wanted to turn off the lights
And step outside as if office hours
Were over. I read, that night, about
The patron saint of the spastic,
How St. Vitus entered, as namesake,
The medical hall of fame.
I followed, for two years, the box scores
For neurological diseases—

Which ones pitched no hitters,
Which ones could be reached for runs.
I learned the spasm variations
By speed, body part, and the chances
To quiet: Dystonia.
Athetosis. Myoclonus.
Nothing at all like *ectoplasm*
Or *miasma*, the cornball, possession
Language of Poe, for whom, among
Others, I put medicine aside.

Now, a student who can't sit still
Insists he's transcribed lists of words
From H. P. Lovecraft because
He's the world's greatest writer.
"*Necrosis. Mephitic*," he reads
From the notebook he's holding.
"Nobody else could think of these,"
He tells me, greatness by way
Of medical dictionaries,
And I blurt *emesis* and *lavage*,
Two ways, offhand, to rid characters
Of the possession of poisons.
And when he twitches and writhes,
Silent, I say *poikilothermia*,
Which sits him still. "Lovecraft's syndrome,"
I add, "very rare. In warm weather
He wore a jacket, something like
A pitcher on the basepaths."

He wrote it down, then, while I spelled,
And I imagined him writing

A story: "The Man Who Was Never Warm,"
Calling him Kjell or Tor, the names
He would give to someone possessed
By an anomaly for mammals,
Nothing as common as the heating
Problems of our old classroom, where,
All winter, we were hot or cold.
In January, a boy returned
From the onomatopoeia
Of whooping cough. In February,
A girl came back from the emblem
Of scarlet fever. We made
Butcher paper banners in art,
Draped them the length of the blackboard
Above where the movie screen scrolled down.
WELCOME BACK, each one said, plus
Our hand-scrawled names. In April,
The Pirates opening in New York,
The room so hot we ran the colors
With sweat, we hung a banner for
The boy with poliomyelitis.
He swung through the door on crutches.
We yelled "Welcome back, Walter,"
Screaming like the possessed, and he
Twitched and jerked, sagged so suddenly
To the floor he turned us into
A phantasmagoria of stone.

Like She Was One of Us

This Thanksgiving, I went back
to my home-for-the-holidays
college sites, driving past houses
where I'd dreaded the draft
with friends. I didn't knock
on any doors to find out
which parents had died, which
had been moved by disease
or age, but I parked at one
leveled corner where I'd spent
a Saturday drinking upstairs
with a high school friend
and his fiancée who still
slept at home. No parents
I knew rented four rooms
over their business, but
they lived for that grocery,
the literal mom and pop
of that defeated street,
and I drank all of the beer
they offered until I fell
asleep on the floor of their store
when I wandered downstairs
for chips. What was I thinking,
a month later, at the wedding,
when their daughter pledged
something impossible
to a statue of Mary?

I was drinking their beer
for the last time, getting
a start on end-of-the-60s
parties I'd come home to,
but her mother matched us
drink for drink and danced
until she fell face first
on the fire hall floor, saying
"Oh shit," like she was one of us.
And Christ, what was she doing
tumbling drunk at the feet
of her son-in-law's friends?
She could have been sensing
the tumor that would kill her
the following winter, the summer
stroke that was fitting itself
to her husband's brain.
Instead, she was afraid
we were dying, not one of us
killed in action although
we believed it was coming, too,
how our parents would outlive us,
our timing wrong, the rubble
of neighborhoods something
we'd see elsewhere, not
at home, not years later,
shamed by staring at vacancy.

The Hitler Dance

After the two of us groaned, after
we turned from the television,
the draft lottery at fifty-six,
three veterans bought us drinks
to toast our coming time
to save democracy. It was 1972,
and those vets got up and did
the Hitler Dance to show us
which fools we needed to erase
from this world, their steps as stiff
and silly as Hitler's just off
the train in surrendered France.
We'd seen the cartoon Führer,
a preview, they said, of one
we'd watch if we were too afraid
to fight. Stand up, they said.
Stand up, stand up, stuttering
like Hitler's boots, not dancing
at all, his small leap of triumph
run over and over in the film loop
technique of propaganda,
something we'd already learned
from television, a commercial
full of happy cats performing
the cha-cha of pleasure near
the processed scraps of the butcher.

The Central Heating of The Kitchen Stove

In the house beside the funeral home,
My wife's family gathered for the first day
Of viewing. All morning, Dziadush had been
Working his wife perfect while his daughters
And sons drank local brands of wine and beer
In the unheated rooms as if they were
Tailgating, late in the season, for death.
I held my Genesee. I slid my three
Ritz crackers onto the warped windowsill
For someone to find, cursing the waster,
After I was hours south. I listened to
Uncle Ed explain the central heating
Of the kitchen stove, four burners on high
Because it was zero in Buffalo,
And he wasn't paying the Arab's rate
For fuel. "I got the oven for backup,"
He said. "There's water to boil for steam."
We toured the living room so cold I checked
For a damaged roof. My wife wished us back
In Pittsburgh; her uncles, in topcoats, split
The seam of one more case. And just after
Aunt Marsha, before she retrieved her heels,
Said I was so tall I must be standing
On God's soapbox, we slipped through the side door
Built in the master bedroom and entered
The tropical weather for proper grief.
So thin from the cancer diet, so rouged,

Busia's face made my wife think, a moment,
The viewing we'd chosen was wrong; I saw
Our names on flowers so unfamiliar
I looked straight ahead in shame. A block west,
Lake Erie creaked. I could walk, I whispered,
The ice to Canada, and three men turned
To say it couldn't possibly be done.

The Insulation of Steam

All round, my father, three months
From bypass, plays best ball of two.
"Four," he writes, "five" and "four" again,
Keeping the line score of selective play.
At seventeen, I stand a sixth time
In sand, ten strokes behind, ground
My glare of wedge like a dare.

This morning, on television,
someone explained the success
of fire walkers. The coals
make bad conductors; there are
calluses and dust and sweat.

On eighteen, while we wait, following
A foursome stalled by water balls,
My father shows me scars, the lines
And dots of surgery. He tops
His first iron, lofts his second
To the near-island of green,
One more par before I take his bag,
And he walks, to save his spikes,
To protect his socks as well,
Barefoot across the parking lot.

In the Liedenfrost Effect,
the reporter said, sweat turns
to an insulation of steam.

For a moment, we're enchanted,
sizzle a swift walk of dreams.

My father doesn't hurry. In the sun,
He says, there's a difference between
Asphalt and cement, using a tone
So placid I free one hand, lay it
To the summer surface and listen,
Like the deaf, for the music of the earth.

The Personal Effects of Antiquity

The doctor, this morning, scrapes wax
From deep in my ear. She carves the prisoner's
Slow tunnel with sharp steel as if sound
Could be restored by danger. "Trust me,"
She says, and shows me, a minute later,
Pictures of the personal effects
Of antiquity: Tweezers, file, toothpick,
Ear scoop—each of them were molded
From metal by Romans. These things,
She says, were perfected early.
The Maya, she adds, so much loved
Crossed eyes, they hung small beads
In front a child's face to induce them.
The Incas adored flat foreheads,
Pressed, until they were three years old,
Their infants' heads with boards.
I tell her about the tattoos on the caveman
In Italy preserved by glacier
For seven thousand years; I tell her
My sons ignore the truth of permanent ink.
And worse, a boy we both know come home
With skull implants, taking anesthesia
To build a metal Mohawk, those poles
Rising from front to back, adjustable,
Pushing up the skin like the pustules
Of the present tense of makeup.
We might as well be spouting "Do this,
Do that" in the Simon Says of beauty,

Calling up the eroticism
Of the inner ear, tongue and breath
Reaching the delicate nerves for sound,
But she says thousands of women,
Because the toxic consequences
Of lead-based makeup took years,
Kept coating their faces, recalling
The crone of changed focus, how beauty,
In the famous trick art, turns into
Illusion hag. Point of view,
I say, but she turns another page,
And both of us confess our wonder
At the mirror which reflected,
Long ago, designs from its own
Unsilvered surface. Like seeing the moon's
Dark side exposed on the blue screen
Of twilight's sky. Like believing.
No matter the ancient Chinese trick
Was explained, at last, by microscope.
Our eyes, unaided, detect nothing,
So we cannot be convinced.

The End of Uncertainty

Researchers are said to have golden hands
when experiments produce a result only for them.

During our two-week retreat, we campers
Had to be praying by sunrise, alone,
Then together, and never for ourselves
Before hymns by the lake where the cold fog
Clung like God's contempt for our indifference.
Our counselor, when we slept in, told us
The tale of St. Cuthbert, who sank neck-deep
In the sea to prepare himself for prayer.
Thanks be to God for the monk who followed,
He said; more thanks for his early rising
And his careful recording of such faith.
He showed us, that morning, his Widow's Mite
And his authentic splinter from the cross.
Because the holiness of parts could keep
Us whole. Because, at night, he kept his fists
Closed in sleep, his fingers curled around them
With Christian discipline, what we could learn
So we'd never worry about God's fire
Or the cyanide of the gas chamber
That had punished the sins of Caryl Chessman.

There were capital punishments, he said,
For countries, the recent executions
Of the French Sudan and Belgian Congo.
Think what's happened to the Gold Coast,
He said, and we waited until he breathed

"Ghana" like the amen at the end of prayer.
His last sermon explained how the world's maps
Were revised and revised until they were
As reliable as The Vinland Map,
Forged to give Vikings credit for first claim
Of discovery. And there were further frauds,
He preached, naming none, but I could tell him,
Today, how Libya, finally, produced
A map without England, expanding
The North Sea to excise what it loathed.
And I could name the astronomer who,
For love of belief, altered photographs
Which proved additional galaxies.

This year the Shroud of Turin is making
A comeback tour while someone claims he owns
The armor worn by Joan of Arc, its nicks
And scratches where her sacred wounds would be.
Soon there may be a whole host of returns:
Piltdown Man, Cardiff Giant, and Barnum's
Colorado Man, all of them called out
Like the planted sick of a faith healer's
Audience. This week, from the riverbank
A mile from here, a skeleton unearthed,
Each day regaining more of itself from
Six fillings and the evidence of wounds.
This morning, the published photographs
Of the long-missing woman, interviews
With her parents, nothing like armor
Keeping their daughter from harm. It's the end
Of uncertainty, the mother declares.

Of uncertainty, the mother declares.
It's the end of miracles, father adds,
Continued on the page where a woman
Displays one thousand origami cranes
She owns to bring fulfillment of wishes.

And I'm thinking, now, that we should forgive
The scientists who have doctored data,
Forgive the golden hands of researchers.
Absolve the man who marked mice with the ink
Of false verification and pardon
The doctor who beat probability
With a simple shift of answers. For they
Do the work of our wishes. For they bring
Miracles and divine intervention.
There are so many God-signs in science
We need a library for likely fraud,
Space enough for enormous paper flocks
To dream among, letting go of no coins
Or splinters, and willing the body not
To shift in sleep, those frail, paper birds so
Securely settled they will not startle.

About the Author

Gary Fincke directs the Writers' Institute at Susquehanna University, where he is a professor of English and also coaches the Susquehanna men's tennis team. He is the author of six book-length collections of poetry, four chapbooks, and two short-story collections. He grew up in a blue-collar area of Pittsburgh and was educated at Kent State University, Miami University of Ohio, and Thiel College. He has won two Pushcart Prizes, six Pennsylvania Council on the Arts fellowships, a PEN Syndicated Fiction Prize, and the Bess Hokin Prize from *Poetry*. His poetry, fiction, and nonfiction have appeared in such places as *The Paris Review*, *Harpers*, *Yankee*, *Newsday*, and *Shenandoah*.